Child Brain Injury
Trust
'hope for tomorrow - today'

CW00890745

Rearrange your brain

by

Sarah Mackie

rearrange

Copyright © 2016 by Sarah Mackie.

All rights reserved. No part of this publication may be reproduced, distributed or transmitted in any form or by any means, including photocopying, recording, or other electronic or mechanical methods, without the prior written permission of the publisher, except in the case of brief quotations embodied in critical reviews and certain other non-commercial uses permitted by copyright law. For permission requests, write to the publisher, addressed "Attention: Permissions Coordinator", at the address below.

Child Brain Injury Trust
Unit 1
Great Barn
Baynards Green Farm
Nr Bicester
Oxfordshire
OX27 7SG

Phone: 01869 341075
Email: info@cbituk.org
Web: www.childbraininjurytrust.org.uk

Publisher's Note: This is a work of fiction. Names, characters, places, and incidents are a product of the author's imagination. Locales and public names are sometimes used for atmospheric purposes. Any resemblance to actual people, living or dead, or to businesses, companies, events, institutions, or locales is completely coincidental.

Book design © Frisbee Creative

Ordering Information: Special discounts are available on quantity purchases by corporations, associations, and others. For details, contact the publisher at the address above.

Oxfordshire /Sarah Mackie /Child Brain Injury Trust — First Edition

ISBN 978-0-9932175-1-7

Printed in the United Kingdom

Introduction

I was delighted to have been selected by The Child Brain Injury Trust to write this book and was inspired by the young people I spoke to who have acquired a brian injury (ABI), or are living with a sibling who has an ABI.

When asked what was the one piece of advice they would give to other siblings their answer was overwhelmingly "everything will be alright in the end."

It was such an emphatic answer, even when things in their lives appeared to me to be incredibly challenging. So it was this resounding optimism that became the bedrock of the book.

My research then led me to speak to some of the Child Brain Injury Trust's experts where I discovered the importance of acknowledging the bad or scary feelings that can often overwhelm us, making it difficult to move on.

So the book is based on a foundational principle of cognitive behavioural therapy that encourages readers to take a moment to consider a situation from a more positive viewpoint to help to impact negative thoughts, feelings and behaviours. We recognise that siblings of children with acquired brain injury are often faced with difficult or overwhelming situations. Learning a strategy that focuses on thinking differently about these challenges, may help children and their families to feel differently and ultimately behave differently and we hope with practice, this approach will equip them with a robust strategy that promotes emotional wellbeing throughout life.

Sarah Mackie
Author

How to use this book

Although this book was written for the siblings of children with an ABI the approach depicted within can be used to help anyone facing a confusing or challenging situation. Taking a moment to think about a situation from a different, more positive viewpoint can help to impact negative thoughts, feelings and behaviours.

When reading the story, take a moment to discuss what is happening and how it might make you feel. How a change in perspective can sometimes be difficult and how practicing this way of thinking might be beneficial?

Repeat the 'chorus' out loud and try to commit it to memory so that it can be recalled easily.

Introduce reflection into your daily routine, around the meal table or in the car on the way home from school, reframing things that might feel embarrassing or difficult. Encourage every member of the family or group to be involved as even trivial things can add up to stress. This can also add an element of humour and reinforce that things one person finds stressful, may not affect others i.e. untidy rooms, wet towels on the floor, lack of a parking space etc.

In especially difficult situations where panic is setting in, try repeating the chorus identifying the bad things and then the good but making them rhyme. This exercise is a little more challenging and can help to occupy the mind.

Acknowledgements

A very special thank you to all those people who helped us develop this book:
Tracey; Ben; Heidi; Emily; Marcus; Joanne, Eve; Grace; Eloise & Callie.

Thank you to Louise Wilkinson of the Child Brain Injury Trust
for project managing the publication of this book.

We would also like to thank the Big Lottery Fund Wales,
Gilbert and Eileen Edgar Foundation, Mackintosh Foundation
and Sir Jules Thorn Trust who have kindly funded the production
and supply of this publication.

**ARIENNIR GAN Y LOTERI
LOTTERY FUNDED**

We learnt about our brains today,
I'd rather have gone out to play.
The way we view the world you see,
Can all be down to you and me.

At last at home,
    with homework done,
We can go out
    and have some fun.
The sun is bright,
    the air is clear,
It's good to have
    my mates just here.

Then off he goes,
   with all his friends,
Will he be back?
   Well, that depends.
I mustn't go,
   'cause I'm not cool,
Don't make a scene,
   that is the rule!

3

It's getting late,
    I hang about,
But then, one of his
    friends shouts out!
"Your brother slipped,
    he's hurt his head,"
My legs go numb,
    I'm full of dread.

There's lots of blood,
   he's not to move,
His mates just stare,
   nowt left to prove.
Can't go with,
   but can't stay here,
What I should do
   just isn't clear.

Then someone goes to get my mum,
My head's like mush, I must be dumb.
Then somewhere down from deep inside,
What I should do? There is a guide…

Remember what the teacher said?
How you feel is in your head!
So close my eyes, try to be calm,
Ignore the sweat that's in my palm.

I feel confused,
Cos things are strange;
I need my brain,
To rearrange...

He's getting help,
  my mum is here,
The A&E is somewhere
  near.
They've given him
  some pain relief,
So feeling bad,
  would have been brief.

My mum's been gone
    for days and days,
Sits by his bed,
    while he just lays.
No one tells me
    anything,
I've only hope
    on which to cling.

Nan's talking with
    a funny voice,
Don't want to stay,
    but I've no choice.
Can't be with Mum,
    cos I'm not grown,
Just waiting here
    sat by the phone.

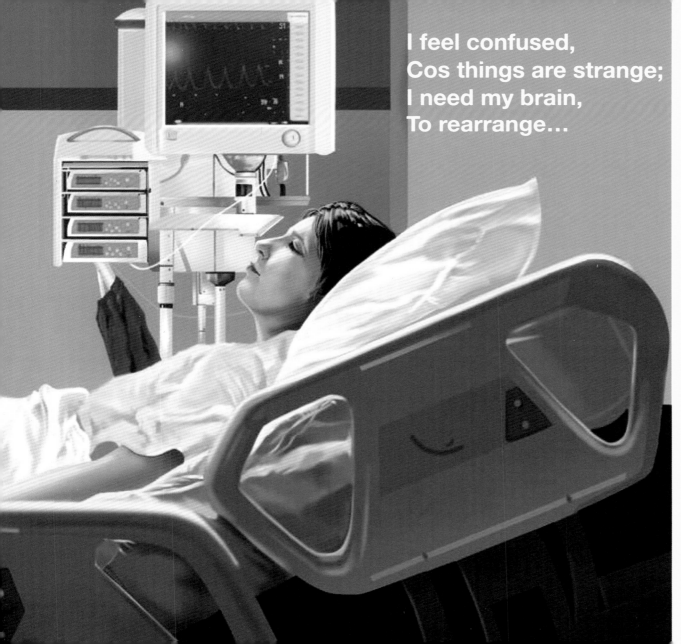

I feel confused,
Cos things are strange;
I need my brain,
To rearrange...

The doctor told me
everything,
Feel so relieved,
I want to sing.
They're keeping him
asleep right now,
It helps to heal his
brain somehow.

11

He's sitting up,
   he stares at me,
Awake at last,
   oh can it be?
But something's off,
   he's not quite right,
Perhaps it's just,
   the room's too bright.

His speech is slow,
   he tires easy,
To make it worse,
   I feel quite queasy.
He's still my brother,
   course he is,
But his look,
   just isn't his.

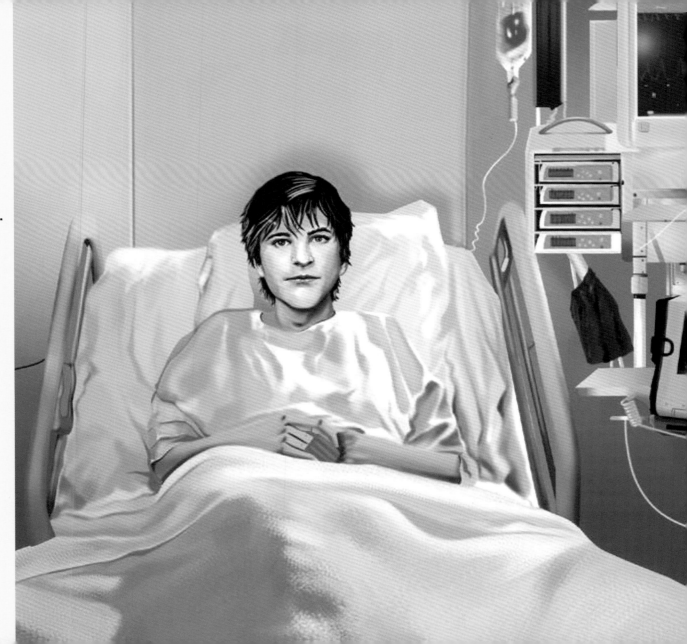

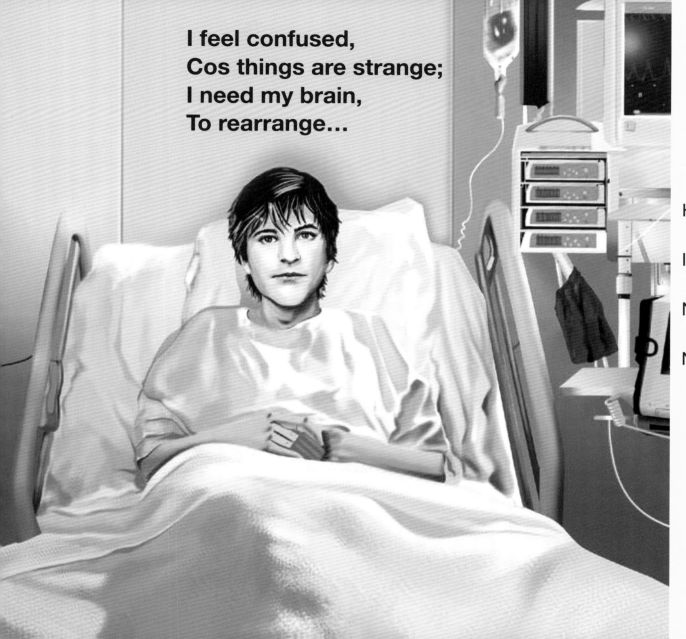

I feel confused,
Cos things are strange;
I need my brain,
To rearrange...

He's woken up,
  it's early days,
In healing speak,
  just the first phase.
Now I can see he's
  getting better,
Next time I'll bring
  his favourite sweater.

13

At last it's time to bring him home,
There's lots of fuss, I mustn't moan.
All his friends around the house,
I'm to be quiet, like a mouse.

The people they just come and come,
The living room is like a scrum!
I can't watch the television,
Mum says sulking's my decision!

I feel confused,
Cos things are strange;
I need my brain,
To rearrange…

At least we're all
    back home together,
Nan's back talking
    'bout the weather.
My brother's really on
    the mend,
So thank you cards
    I'll help him send.

15

Could he be getting
    more attention?
More presents?
We'll need an extension!
To top it all he's got
    some drums,
To help him when
    frustration comes.

These tempers come
    so very fast,
My feelings,
    always coming last.
He shouts without
    apology,
But what about
    my sanity?

I feel confused,
Cos things are strange;
I need my brain,
To rearrange...

Yet I can still go out
   to play,
And at my friend's house
   I can stay.
Auditioned for the
   school production,
Because for me,
   there's no obstruction.

Out in public, feeling weird,
Staring eyes, worse than I feared.
Spot some of my friends from school,
They drop their heads, I feel a fool.

Now he tries to eat a burger,
There's such a mess left for our server.
My cheeks are red, please let's go home,
At least there, all he does is moan.

I feel confused,
Cos things are strange;
I need my brain,
To rearrange…

Wait a minute, that's not fair,
He's learning, and it's rude to stare!
I dip my chips into my sauce,
I smear my face; Mum looks quite cross.

To my surprise, she does the same,
"How 'bout we make it, a new game?
Come on, you've only eaten half!"
Got to admit; feels good to laugh.

Can you believe?
    A brand new puppy!
Most I got?
    A yellow guppy!
Mum says he needs it,
    for his brain,
And he must take
    the time to train.

The ugly thing
    chews all my stuff,
I yelled so loud,
    I'm out of puff!
It wees on shoes,
    just here and there,
At this rate,
    I will have no hair!

I feel confused,
Cos things are strange;
I need my brain,
To rearrange...

The dog is cute,
    it likes a cuddle,
My bedroom is
    less of a muddle.
My brother's working
    hard to train,
Even walking down
    the lane.

I can see they're
    making progress,
Cos his problems,
    seem to show less.
I know that things
    won't be the same,
Just pleased that we
    can play again.

Friday night, is the big show,
Got tickets, so they all could go.
But they've got a late appointment,
I can't hide my disappointment.

"WHY NOT ME FOR ONCE?" I yell,
"Nan will come; sure you'll do well."
There's just no point, she isn't thinking,
Holding back my tears by blinking.

I feel confused,
Cos things are strange;
I need my brain,
To rearrange...

The play went well,
 they made some tapes,
So there's no need
 for sour grapes.
They laughed and cheered,
 said I was great,
Even let me stay up late.

23

My brother's also
    doing well,
His injuries now
    hard to tell.
The doctors said that
    he's much better,
They even liked his
    Irish Setter.

So this is now
    my family,
Crazy and loud
    as can be.
Drums and dogs
    all in the mix,
Really nothing left to fix.

My brother's had to
    learn some stuff,
That second time,
    seems rather tough.
But all that we can do
    is try,
Now you have skills,
    you can apply.

This is life,
    most times it's great,
But I will have to
    tell you straight.
Even when you get
    a fright,
I'll tell you now,
    you'll be alright.

Remember what the
    teacher said...
How you feel is in
    your head.
Just rearrange
    the things you see,
And cool and calm
    you'll always be.

26